Novels for Students, Volume 4

27500 Drake Rd.
Farmington Hills, MI 48331-3535

ISBN 0-7876-2114-5
ISSN 1094-3552

Printed in the United States of America.
10 9 8 7 6 5 4 3

July's People

Nadine Gordimer

1981

Introduction

In light of the uprisings of the 1970s, Nadine Gordimer presented a very bleak and cynical prophecy to white and black South Africa. That prophecy suggested no solution to problematic race relations but foresaw an inevitable overthrow of the apartheid system of the Afrikaner Nationalists. With the declaration of independence by the neighboring nations of Angola, Mozambique, and Zimbabwe, the demise of white rule in South Africa was anticipated.

July's People takes place during a future revolution in South Africa. Amid such chaos, traditional roles are overturned and new ones must be forged. In that sense, the novel exists in Antonio Gramsci's (the source of the novel's epigraph) interregnum—between the explosion of the old but before the birth of the new.

July's People captures the mood of a South Africa expecting revolutionary violence just like that experienced by neighboring countries. Instead of writing about a revolution, however, the novel assumes such an event will happen and imagines what affect it might have on a liberal white family. In this case, the family decides to accept their servant's offer of refuge and flee to his village. There, with all the awkwardness of Friday nursing Robinson Crusoe, they hope to wait out the war. Gradually, all the family's accoutrements of civilization are given up, stolen, or proven to be completely useless. Simultaneously, the power relations of society are revealed as hollow. However, there is hope in that self-awareness and in the children's immersion in village life as a possible route to the construction of a new South Africa.

Author Biography

Gordimer was born in Springs, an East Rand mining town outside Johannesburg in the Transvaal region of South Africa, in 1923. Springs served as the setting of her first novel, *The Lying Days* (1953). Her father was a jeweler from Latvia and her mother was of British descent. Growing up, Gordimer was often sequestered indoors because her mother feared she had a weak heart. She spent some time in convent school where, she admits in an autobiographical essay "A Bolter and the Invincible Summer" (1963), she was a habitual truant.

In response to her confinement, Gordimer began writing at the age of nine. Her first published story was "The Quest for Seen Gold," which appeared in June of 1937 in the *Johannesburg Sunday Express.* Fortunately, she maintains, the publication of her work did not lead to the smothering that one sees with those considered "gifted." Instead she was left to her own devices and, thus, began a long career of writing about life in South Africa.

Her short stories were continually published in magazines until her first book came out in 1952. It was a collection of short stories titled *The Soft Voice of the Serpent* (1952). Already, her technique was evident. Her writing had clarity, little emotion, and great control.

Gordimer lived through the system of Apartheid and fought to bring about its end. She was a member of the African National Congress (which was an illegal party until the 1980s), and she chose to stay in South Africa when many other writers and political dissidents left for school or safety in Europe and America. However, she was not a prominent dissident—like Ruth First—but she was a voice of protest. "I remain," she said, "a writer, not a public speaker: nothing I say here will be as true as my fiction." Still, many of her books were banned in South Africa from 1958 until 1991.

A prolific writer, Gordimer has written many essays on politics, censorship, writing, and other writers. Much of this work parallels her fictional work and taken together she has painted a damning picture of apartheid. She was a founding member of the Congress of South African Writers. She has won numerous awards for her writing, including the Booker prize, the Modern Literature Association Award, and the Bennett Award. Many universities have honored her with degrees and the French government gave her the decoration of Officier de l'Ordre des Arts et des Lettres. In 1991, she was awarded the Nobel Prize for Literature. Currently, she lives in South Africa, is the Vice President of PEN (a worldwide organization of writers), a member of the Congress of South African Writers, and she continues to write.

Plot Summary

In *July's People*, Nadine Gordimer depicts the lives of a liberal, white South African family, the Smales, forced to flee to the native village of their black servant, July. Gordimer sets her novel during a fictional civil war in which black South Africans violently overturn the system of apartheid. In order to escape the violence in Johannesburg, the Smales must accept July's charity and live a life that makes them all confront their assumptions about one another.

The novel opens the morning after an exhausting three-day trip through bush country to reach the village. July brings tea for Maureen and Bamford Smales and breakfast for their children, Victor, Gina, and Royce. After experiencing disorientation from the trip, Maureen asks her husband about their vehicle, a small truck called a bakkie. He tells her that July has hidden it.

The Smales find themselves dependent on July, and July's family questions their presence in the village. He explains the their situation, telling his mother and wife, Martha, about the violence in the country. They cannot, however, fully believe his account given their past experience with white dominance.

To do something other than listen constantly for news on his radio, Bam Smales builds a water tank for the village. Maureen tries to read a novel, since July will not let her work, but discovers that no fiction can compete with her current situation. She then recalls her girlhood days and remembers walking home from school with her family's black servant, Lydia, who carried Maureen's school case on her head. One day, a photographer took their picture. Years later, Maureen saw the picture in a *Life* photograph book and for the first time questioned why Lydia was carrying her books.

One night, after Bam unsuccessfully tries socializing with the villagers, Bam and Maureen are startled by July's departure as a passenger in the bakkie. Anxious over losing the vehicle, they argue, blaming each other for their situation. Later, while standing nude in the rain, Maureen sees the bakkie return. She falls asleep that night without telling Bam about the vehicle.

When July comes to their hut the next day, Bam greets him with the inappropriate authority of their former relationship. Apparently ignoring Bam's tone, July tells them he went to the shops for supplies. Though they could, they do not ask him for the keys to the bakkie. July begins to learn how to drive. When the they ask him what he will do if caught driving the vehicle, he says he will say he owns it.

Later, Maureen returns the bakkie's keys to July. Knowing that she does not want him to keep the keys, he makes her recall his former status as her "boy" when he kept the keys to her house. He also recalls the distrust he sensed from her at the time. Stung by his words, Maureen tries to defend her treatment of him and says their former relationship has ended, that he is no longer a servant. He then shocks her by asking if she is going to pay him this month. He offers the car keys back to her, saying he worked for her for fifteen years because his family needed him to. She then retaliates by mentioning Ellen, his mistress in Johannesburg. Though feeling a hollow victory, Maureen knows July will never forgive her this transgression. He keeps the car keys.

Bam kills two baby wart-hogs with his small shotgun. During the hunt, he offers to let his black hunting companion, Daniel, shoot the gun sometime. Bam gives the larger wart-hog to the villagers and keeps the smaller (and more tender) one. Everyone joyfully feasts on the meat, an intoxicating delicacy, and Bam and Maureen make love for the first time since their journey.

The scene shifts to July and his family eating the meat and talking about the Smales. July discounts Martha's worries that the white family will bring trouble. Martha recalls the times without July when he, like most men with families, worked in the city. Like the seasons, the long absences of their husbands have become an expected part of black women's lives.

Gina and her friend, Nyiko, play with newborn kittens, and Maureen scolds them. Later, after they listen for news on the radio, Bam asks Maureen if she found a home for the kittens. She reveals that she has drowned them in a bucket of water.

Maureen tries working with the women in the fields, digging up leaves and roots. Afterward, she goes to see July, who is working on the bakkie. July does not want to hear about the killing on the news and hopes everything "will come back all right." Maureen asks, dumbfounded, if he really wants a return to the ways things were. July asks if hunger compels her to search for spinach with the women; she replies that she goes to pass the time. As always, she feels that the workplace language they speak hinders their ability to communicate.

When July says she should not work with the women, she asks if he fears she will tell his wife about Ellen. He angrily asserts that she can only tell Martha that he has always been a good servant. Maureen, frightened, realizes that the dignity she thought she had always conferred upon him was actually humiliating to him. He informs her that he and the Smales have been summoned to the chief's village. Though July has authority in his village, they still must ask the chief's permission to stay. Maureen struggles with her new subservience to July.

The Smales visit the chief the next morning, afraid that the chief will force them out. The chief asks them why they have come to his nation and asks about events in Johannesburg. He cannot believe that the white government is powerless and that whites are running from blacks. He says that the black revolutionaries are not from his nation and that the whites, who would never let him own a gun, will give him guns to aid in the struggle against the black attackers. He tells Bam to bring his gun and teach him how to shoot it.

Outraged by this suggestion, Bam asks if the chief really intends to kill other blacks, saying that the entire black nation is the chief's nation. After further discussion, the chief allows them to stay with Mwawate (July) and says that he will visit them to learn how to shoot Bam's gun.

On the return trip, July explains that the chief talks instead of acts. Furthermore, the chief, who never fought the whites, is too poor and defenseless to fight other blacks. Upon their return to their hut, Maureen and Bam speak in the phrases they had used in their former life, and these phrases cannot adequately describe their current predicament. Bam begins criticizing July's new confidence and his criticisms of the chief. Maureen says that July was talking about himself, that he will not fight for anyone and is risking his life by having the family there. Maureen suggests that they leave, making Bam confront what they both know: they have nowhere to go and no means by which to get there.

With the women, Maureen clumsily cuts grass for the huts. After the cutting, July criticizes Martha for placing the grass bundles in front of the Bam and Maureen's house, where their children will ruin it. They discuss July's past and his times in the city over the last fifteen years. Rejecting July's contention that his family will move to the city once the fighting ends, Martha suggests that he stay in the village. According to Daniel, they will no longer face white restrictions, and, with his city experience, July can run his own shop.

A man brings a battery-operated amplifier to the village and provides them with a night's entertainment, during which many villagers drink heavily. The Smales do not partake in the drinking but return to their hut, where they find their gun missing.

With no police to help him, Bam is impotent in the face of the theft. Maureen feels humiliated for Bam. She leaves to find July, who is by the bakkie. They realize that only Daniel was absent from the party, and Maureen says July must get the gun from him. Daniel, however, has left. After July asserts that the Smales always make trouble for him, Maureen accuses July of stealing small items from her in Johannesburg. Angered, he speaks to her in his own language, and "She understood although she knew no word. Understood everything: what he had had to be, how she had covered up to herself for him, in order for him to be her idea of him. But for himself—to be intelligent, honest, dignified for *her* was nothing; his measure as a man was taken elsewhere and by others," his own people. July then informs her that Daniel has joined the revolution. She tells July that he abandoned Ellen and only wants the bakkie so he can feel important, but that, too, will become useless when his gas money runs out.

After Gina goes to play with Nyiko and Bam goes with Victor and Royce to fish, a helicopter with unidentifiable markings flies over the village. Maureen fervently chases the helicopter, and the novel ends with her still running toward it and its unknown occupants, who could be either "saviours or murderers."

Characters

The chief

The chief, as befits his position, is the only character who attempts to make sense of the greater picture. He has no weapons and no wealth. He asks Bam for his gun; however, Bam is shocked that the chief would kill the "good guys"—the people of Mandela and Sobukwe—for the white government. But at least the chief wants to do something even if alone and armed with one gun. He would prefer action to hiding out and waiting to be taken over again. What Bam does not want to understand is that the chief and his people have their own history which has little in common with the urban African National Congress.

Daniel

July's friend Daniel shows him how to drive the bakkie as well as fix it. He befriends the white family. Bam shows him how to shoot and Daniel accompanies the family to the chief. He disappears at the same time that Bam's gun goes missing. It is assumed he has taken the gun and gone off to join the revolutionary army.

Ellen

While July lives with the Smales, he has a mistress named Ellen. She is from Botswana and is an office cleaner. The money she earns in the city is sent to pay for her son's high school education in Soweto. While ironing July's clothes with Maureen's iron, she sometimes chats with Maureen. "[O]nce [she] had put a hand under her breasts with the gesture with which women declare themselves in conscious control of their female destiny … I'm sterilized at the clinic."

July

July recalls the character of Friday in the eighteenth-century novel by Daniel Defoe, *Robinson Crusoe.* Benevolent masters named both characters for calendar measurements and both were trusted with their masters' lives. July appears to be "their servant, their host," but the revolution has disrupted traditional roles. He remains the white family's savior, but as time goes on they become his people. He represents all the myths and stereo-types of the black servant, but he also uses those same myths to his advantage.

Determined to remain their servant as long as he is paid, July seeks to become the master of the family. It is a revolution of roles rather than the herald of a new society. July accomplishes his objective by sequestering them and confining them to their role as his master. As such, they depend on him for everything. He also makes sure that Maureen is unable to establish relations with the other women and, therefore, she cannot fully integrate to society. Lastly, July slowly appropriates the tokens of civilization they have managed to bring with them, the most important being the bakkie.

Lydia

In a flashback, Maureen returns to her young love for a family servant named Lydia. She recalls with joy the many afternoons that she would "bump" into Lydia on the way home from school. Customarily, Lydia would take Maureen's burden onto her head with the shopping and they would go home. The relationship is one of master and servant. However, in Maureen's memory it is also that of young girl in love with an older female. From this context she is able to say that the photo, taken by the journalist to depict apartheid as a white girl next to a "black woman with the girl's school case on her head," shows a context of "affection and ignorance." The memory of Lydia reveals Maureen's blindness to her own empowered status.

Martha

The wife of July, Martha is a simple character. She represents the agrarian traditional figure that is resigned to her role. For her, "The sun rises, the moon sets; the money must come, the man must go." She does not react to the white people in her mother's house too much nor does she relate to Maureen. The women met and "something might have come of it. But not much."

Mwawate

See July

Nyiko

A girl from the village who becomes Gina's childhood intimate. They become more and more inseparable and are reminded of their origins of difference only when the adults want to know whose child Gina is minding. She is a subject of fascination for Bam and Maureen when she takes a sausage.

Bamford Smales

Descended from Boers (Dutch colonists), Bam has the privilege of the white South African in an Apartheid state. He is an architect for Caprano & Partners and husband to Maureen. He likes to boast of being a judge at conferences and of his professional abilities, like speaking French. He also name-drops. Being middle class, he hunts for sport and bought himself the yellow bakkie as a hunting vehicle. He sees himself as strong, masculine, and in control of his life. He does not mind exchanging suburban leisure for laboring on improvements about the village. In his mind this gives him an importance, but in reality he is a secondary character to his employers and to his wife.

Politically, Bam is a pacifist who empathizes with the blacks. Personally, the situation utterly emasculates him; his former servant controls the bakkie and calls the shots. He admits that he feels like "a boy with a pea-shooter." His final abdication as white man occurs when his gun is stolen. Without his gun he is of no use to the chief, he holds no symbolic power, and he is unable to uphold his economic place of provider and, therefore, has no sexual claim on Maureen.

Media Adaptations

- *July's People* was made into an audio cassette by Blackstone Audio Books in 1993.

Gina Smales

Of all the characters, only Gina represents the

hope of that a new South Africa is possible. She shows the opposite characteristics of the small-minded Victor. She is the second child and shows every sign of ease with village life. She finds a best friend in Nyiko and a sense of responsibility in minding the younger children in the village. In addition, she begins to learn the local language. The beginning of a new South African person can be glimpsed in Gina—she is multilingual and the race barrier that her brother Victor depends on is not present for her. Gina insists on her difference from her siblings. Her mother notices she is "always a moody bastard" who acts like a witch to her brothers.

Maureen Hetherington Smales

The focus of the novel, Maureen is a woman from the Western Area Gold Mines who has been living in the safe environs of the suburbs. Until the revolution and the flight to July's village, she was in charge of her household and family. Her husband was a wonderfully successful architect and they both shared a liberal view of apartheid. Together they hoped that dialogue and discussion would bring about greater equality.

All of that vanishes in the flight in the yellow bakkie with her family and servant to the countryside. Leaving her suburban life behind, she attempts to manufacture a new value system within her new surroundings, but instead discovers that values are relative. Further, those values depend on personal relationships; in her new life, she discovers these relationships are not as strong as she once thought. Eventually, after a failed relationship with July, she runs off into the unknown.

In this final flight, she is finally understands that she must break free from the circularity of her traditional role. Thus by abandoning her family and being spumed by her servant, she virtually joins Daniel and merges with the social revolution.

Royce Smales

Royce is the littlest of the Smales and July's favorite. He annoys his parents with his request for a Coke. He slyly exacerbates his bother's tantrum by asking if he is really going to buy a buggy. He at once questions his brother's awakening masculinity while making light of the moment.

Victor Smales

The oldest child, Victor adamantly tries to maintain racial separation despite the liberal example of his parents. He wants to have the spoils of white rule. The character of Victor represents the idea that racism is childish. Furthermore, the pettiness of the racist is that of a spoiled child who insists on dragging out his racing-car track. This is demonstrated when Victor wants to keep the blacks away from the rain catch his father has made ("who owns the rain?" asks his mother). He is also infuriated that a black should accuse him of stealing garbage—an orange sack. Victor also shows that the anger of a racist person must be handled carefully, " [he] was angry with a white man's anger, too big for him." Yet Victor learns some manners from his black playmates, though not as many as Gina and Royce do. This occurs when he accepts a piece of fishing line from July with the typical open palm gesture of the other children.

Tsatsawani

July's mother gives up her hut for the Smales. She is apprehensive of the white people's presence in the village and resents being unable to replace the roof of her hut. She represents old age, as well as the natural rhythm of the village and its agricultural focus. She also contrasts with the image of Ban's associate who died in his own plane's crash. Grandmother, conversely, is still working and will work "bent lower and lower towards the earth until finally she sank to it—the only death she could afford."

Themes

Body

The incredible situation which the Smales find themselves in is attested to and dealt with at a very personal level. The real discomfort and disruption of the revolution has been displaced to a new awareness of the physical body. "For the first time in her life [Maureen] found that she smelled bad between her legs ... [she] disgustedly scrubbed." There is also a constant concern about living in the village, especially the risk of disease. However, this fear does not stop them from trying to keep up appearances. Maureen secretly washes her menstrual rags in the river because the shame of her period looms far greater than the "risk of bilharzia."

In addition to these sufferings, it is in the description of another person's body that the Smales admit their whiteness. Maureen comments on her children coughing like the black children do. She also notes that her kids look dirtier than the village children because of their white skin. It is never said directly but it is suggested that there is something natural about black people living in primeval nature—they seem to blend in with darkness: "they could see his fingernails and his eyes." These are intentional stereotypical references. But the most certain sign that the family is realizing its fear of losing whiteness (or going native) and becoming villagers is Bam's terrifying report that he has seen Royce wipe himself with a stone—not a treasured piece of toilet paper.

Nature

Reversing roles, the blacks are now able to walk freely in the city, and Maureen feels herself confined to the hut: "Maureen could not walk out into the boundlessness." She excuses her confinement by saying she fears being spotted by a patrol; but everyone knows they are there. Disease keeps her from going to the river too often. She steers clear from July's hut while July keeps her from fraternizing with the other women. She tries to work with the women once in the field—but she feels self-conscious because of her white legs.

Before her flight into the unknown at the end of the novel, the only time she gives into nature is a secret, naked, dance in the rain. Her attitude or fear of the boundlessness is repeated in her attitude toward her own body and those bodies around her. Overcoming nature becomes Maureen's epiphany.

Sex Roles

The disruption of reality—or what Maureen has known as reality—caused by the revolution has forced her to reflect upon the nature of reality, "since that first morning she had become conscious in the hut, she had regained no established point of a continuing present from which to recognize her own sequence." Reality, in this context, had been decided upon in the mind of each individual according to their position in an economy of sex roles. Reality is dependent upon human relations that are based on a false resistance to apartheid and a position of claimed innocence. "The Humane creed ... depended on validities staked on a belief in the absolute nature of intimate relationships between human beings."

Maureen realizes her life has been gilded by a suburbia whose sterility thwarts honest intimacy. It is this realization that causes her to feel embarrassed about Ellen and about visiting July when he was ill. She also realizes that power relations in society are reflected within her family. She discovers that there is little real intimacy and begins to view her husband and children as strangers.

Topics for Further Study

- The ending of July's People leaves a

great deal to the imagination. Imitating Gordimer's style, write your own ending. Was there a helicopter or not?

- Do some research into the disease risks associated with living in the rural regions (as opposed to the wilderness) of South Africa. Given the fact of war and that July's home is an old agricultural village, how much of Maureen's worry about illness is valid? How much is simply an expression of her discomfort at not being in familiar surroundings?
- In the United States we had a similar, though milder, system of laws that institutionalized racial discrimination known as Jim Crow Laws. What were those laws and how would they compare with the system of apartheid?
- Gordimer wrote her novel at a time when a racial revolution seemed inevitable. Americans have felt this fear in the past as well (for example, at the times of The Great Sioux Uprising, Wounded Knee, Watts Riots, LA Riots). Does that fear exist in any form today, say, in immigration quotas or as hysteria over the Mexican border?

Furthermore, her previous conception relied on "sexual love formulated in master bedrooms" for the purposes of fulfilling a "place in the economy." From this viewpoint, her marriage to Bam becomes insupportable. Disgust grows between them in parallel to their individual disgust at their own body. She takes on the "matriarchal frown of necessity performed without question, without reasoning; the same frown she had had turned up to her by July's wife." While he "had the menacing aspect of maleness as man has before the superego has gained control of his body, come out of sleep. His penis was swollen under his rumpled trousers." Not only do bodies disgust them, but also the very physical life of the village disgusts them. Nothing is pressed; nothing is familiar.

The marital breakdown is reflected in the pronouns used toward each other but also in the sexual act. They do not have sex except for the night of the hog feast when they succumb to the influence of the meat. Bam dreams of the pig; he wakes to what he thinks is pig's blood on him when it is her menstrual blood he sees. It is a further sign that they are not in the sterility of the suburb and that their coitus rests on violence—the master bedrooms of apartheid economics.

Likewise, Maureen offers herself to July but "the death's harpy image she made of herself meant nothing to him, who had never been to a motor show complete with provocative girls." It is an awesome conjunction. Marital sex has become an act of drunken violence neither really wanted. Maureen, in her confusion over reality, desperately and pointlessly offers herself to July—the new master of the bakkie—as another possession, the final one. Having now broken all possible connections, marital and otherwise, Maureen is ready to leave.

Culture Clash

Along with natural bodily function, culture clash is a main thematic of the story. An important aspect of this is the way that Maureen and July conjure the legendary friendship of Robinson Crusoe and Friday—but replacing Friday's cheery obedience with a tense political dilemma.

The similarity is found in the careful listing and discussion of objects. In the story of Crusoe, he is incredibly lucky to have been able to recover many items from the shipwreck to assist the creation of a marooned settlement. The most important possessions for the Smales are the bakkie ("A ship that had docked in a far country"), the radio (before which Bam looks like a monkey fingering the bars of a cage), malarial pills, toilet paper, and the gun. Conversely, July's unwanted items from the past—like the two pink glasses of the opening scene—are now employed to recreate the Bam and Maureen's home.

More ironic, however, are the items grabbed in the hectic moment of flight which serve absolutely no purpose: the race track; bundles of monetary notes which become bits of paper; ornamental clay vessels; and "a gadget for taking the dry cleaner's tags off clothes." In reference to these items, Maureen notes that they now have nothing. Then she sees her old scissors and her small knife-grinder in use around the village, realizing that July "must have filched them." It is Maureen's feeling of deprivation of discarded household items that prevents her from seeking July in his hut. "She no more wanted to have to see her cast-off trappings here, where they separated [July] from the way other people lived around him, than she did back there, where they separated him from the way she lived." But while Maureen works through the problem of possession, Bam, on the other hand, is utterly emasculated by the loss of his bakkie and his gun.

Style

Narrative

The narrative is told from a third person point of view and the tone of the narrative voice is that of dispassionate documentation. The voice reports on the activities and behavior of the characters as they adjust to their marooned state. However, the narration does not add information about the world that might explain the situation. In this way, the narrator knows only as much as the Smales know or learn from the radio. At the story's focus is Maureen, her thoughts are more often revealed. As a result, the story told is filtered through her and censored by her body of knowledge. Furthermore, the reader loses track of the political background and must consider what the basis of human relations are and what they need to be in a more just society.

Occasionally the focus shifts to Bam and there is some insight into his thought process; but this is not enough to give him any depth. Maureen and July (who is a function of her) are the only substantial characters in the novel. Maureen causes the narrative's linearity to be clouded in a way that reflects her disbelief that any of the revolution was possible or happening.

Realism

Realism is a literary technique often used to examine the mores and customs of middle-and lower-class characters. *July's People* focuses on middle-class liberal whites to examine them as they deal with a complete disruption of their society. The story asks the question, what next—what kind of role do white people have when they are overthrown? That question is the subtext of Maureen's battle with July. In fact, the climax of the story is the moment when he yells at her in his own language and she understands. She hears that her sympathies for him were an insult, that he is trapped as a servant in a society ruled by whites. But that is his morass.

The real criticism of the story is centered on Maureen. She represents the liberal who tried to prevent or ignore the growing revolutionary violence. Now, she discovers, she must do something. The focus on the hypocrisy of the liberal political stance is exposed without having to resort to a specific listing of their faults. It is exposed by a story of a symbolic family marooned among people it never really wanted to encounter (though they might have felt for them from a distance). Gordimer wants the reader to examine his or her beliefs. The novel's dramatic circumstances serve to point out that only a fantastic event, unfortunately, will wake people up.

Leitmotif

In musical composition, a leitmotif describes

the technique whereby certain themes are repeated to signify emotion, announce a character, or accompany specific scenery. *July's People* is composed of an incredible series of such events whereby the novel's noise—the insects, the radio, the people, the helicopter—becomes a symphony or operatic display. Moreover, every superficial theme actually reinforces the overarching theme that a woman, Maureen, cannot simply hide from history.

There are subtle objects that instantly retell the story. For example, Manzoni's *I Promessi Sposi* is the only novel Maureen has taken with her. She never reads the famous nineteenth-century novel, but it reminds her of civilization. Like that novel, her marriage is thwarted by the overlord July—but there will be no happy ending because she rejects suburban culture with its fanciful tales of romance. Another example is found in the pink teacups and the way July supplies fruit at the end of the meal. The insistence upon living in the same manner as they once did only further points out the absurdity of that previous life.

Historical Context

South Africa

The Union of South Africa was formed in 1910 under a constitution excluding blacks from parliament. In 1912, a number of chiefs joined members of the middle class to form the opposition party, the African National Congress (ANC). ANC protests from 1912 until 1940 were within the law. When WWII broke out, South Africa fought with the Allies. After the war, there was a great influx of Africans into the cities. This shift in demographics, coupled with a rise in crime and shanty-towns, created a degree of paranoia amongst the enfranchised (white) citizens. In the elections of 1948, the Afrikaner Nationalists were voted in because they promised to restore order.

The Afrikaner Nationalists began a system of apartheid, a regime based on racial discrimination that was instituted nationwide. In 1956, for example, the regime removed 60,000 mixed-blood "colored" from the voting rolls of Cape Province. In late summer, 100,000 non-whites were forcibly evicted from their homes to make room for whites. Africans were required to live in designated areas and carry "passes" or permission papers. The inability to provide an inquiring official with one's papers meant jail or fines. Generally, the system of apartheid aimed to keep the non-white people living under South African rule a disciplined pool of workers. Dissent or organization into labor unions or political parties was not tolerated. The political groups, lead by the ANC, used boycotts, strikes, and demonstrations in an effort to change the government.

On March 21, 1960, thousands of people all over South Africa responded to an ANC call of civil disobedience. The people marched without their passes and offered themselves for arrest. The government responded at Sharpeville, 40 miles south of Johannesburg, where 20,000 people had gathered. Police panicked and opened fire. Sixty-nine black people dead, 180 injured, and one week later the ANC was banned. This event forced leaders to flee underground where they formed armed groups whose aim was sabotage. One of the leaders jailed soon after was Nelson Mandela.

Soweto

Tensions increased as the strictures of apartheid tightened: every year saw the passage of laws decreasing the civil liberties of blacks. It also saw the highest incarceration rate in the world and barbaric police brutality. The opposition parties were working underground but were not invisible for long. In the 1970s, the Black Consciousness movement formed but then was destroyed by the government. Its purpose was accomplished; it raised awareness among people and made possible a new generation of black dissidence. A revolt was organized from schools where teachers and students were dissatisfied with low salaries, a crumbling education system, and a recent law that made Afrikaans the equivalent of English.

On June 16, 1976, roughly 15,000 school children turned out to demonstrate against apartheid in Soweto. The police opened fire, killing 25, and wounding dozens more. The protest spread over the country and continued through 1977. One of the organizers was soon arrested. His name was Stephen Biko and his death in jail created an international outcry. After restoring order, the government appointed the Collié Commission of Inquiry to investigate the cause of the unrest in the black residential areas.

The Commission gave its report in February of 1980 and stated that the problem stemmed from the implementation of the language policy and ensuing linguistic misunderstandings. As a result of the report, Soweto was given a new school, teachers were given a raise, and a new Education Act made school compulsory—boycotts and protests were now illegal. What the government did not realize was that Soweto had galvanized a palpable opposition that had not been raised by Sharpeville or any of the other incidents. It is at this point, when "it seemed that all was quieting down again," that Gordimer published *July's People* and the ban on *Burger's Daughter* was lifted.

State of Emergency

The government dealt with Soweto effectively. An independent homeland scheme wherein there would be limited self-governance was masterminded by P. W. Botha and seemed to ease tensions. Meanwhile, some laws were changed and some liberties restored to blacks. White administration of the homelands was ended in 1982. But police actions simultaneously intensified throughout this period. In 1984, a new constitution was written and Botha became president. On the issue of parliaments, a compromise was brokered whereby there would be one lawmaking body but with three racially segregated chambers.

The developments at the parliamentary level translated into frustration at the street level. Youths were impatient for change—they had grown up aware of the Soweto massacre and conscious of the guerilla efforts of the ANC. On September 3, 1984, the day the new Tricameral parliament was to become reality, riots broke out and South Africa entered a constant state of turmoil.

This unrest led to the declaration of a State of Emergency. The army re-enforced the police in October. Then in February 1985, the government tried to remove a squatter camp outside Cape Town called Crossroads. This had been tried before but the task of removing the 87,000 residents had not been achieved. During this attempt, 18 people were killed and international news cameras were on the scene. The whole world saw the violence and leaders around the world were furious. On March 21, 25 years after Sharpeville, the police killed 40 people gathered for a funeral of other police victims.

The End of White Rule

Since 1985, the ANC and its affiliates had become a revolutionary army with increasing tactical sophistication. They attacked government posts, police, and, by 1989, military installations. South Africa was in a state of civil war and the government was losing. The National Party changed its tactics by making F. W. de Klerk leader of the party. De Klerk was an outsider who was more receptive than his predecessors were. He was elected president in 1989. He lifted the ban on the ANC and released Nelson Mandela from jail. Throughout 1990s, exiles returned and new elections were called for. Mandela was elected president in 1994 and incredible change swept the country.

Critical Overview

Gordimer has never had a large reading audience inside South Africa. South Africans have been dissatisfied with her work or they have been kept from it through censorship. Internationally, however, Gordimer has been the interpreter of South Africa through her short stories and novels. *July's People* was hardly different in this respect, but it is often treated not as a novel but as prophecy.

Compare & Contrast

- **South Africa**: in 1991 the total population was about 30 million persons of which 5 million were white, 2.5 million were people of color, and the rest were black. The black population is expected to total 66 million by 2010 with little change in the other two racial categories.
- **USA**: the total population now exceeds 267 million persons. Approximately 11% are black. The birth rate among whites is low but among Hispanics and native Americans it is very high.
- **South Africa**: European colonialists designated 10 areas as reservations for blacks. These areas became

known as homelands and were briefly independent. In 1994, the homelands were reabsorbed during the elections so that South Africa is one administrative unit without a reservation system.

- **USA**: European colonialists signed treaties with Native Americans granting them rights to homelands. This too was a reservation system. These treaties recognize the Indian Tribes as sovereign Nations but the United States has never allowed Native governments much independence.

Soon after its publication, Anne Tyler praised the novel in the *New York Times Book Review*. She compared the story to Daniel Defoe's *Robinson Crusoe* and noted the strange symbols of civilization, like toilet paper. For Tyler, the novel "demonstrates with breathtaking clarity the tensions and complex interdependencies between whites and blacks in South Africa." Joan Silbur agreed in her review in the same magazine. She added that "Gordimer's novel is an intense look at a network of power relations—black to white, servant to master, male to female, child to parent—and the enormous changes wrought in all allegiances once power shifts utterly. For all the extremities of the situation it chronicles and the suspense—drama of its plot, it is a very subtle book—spare, careful, and instructive."

Judith Chettle, however, was not so appreciative in *The National Review.* Understanding that revolution has long been a possibility in the talk of South Africa, she simply sees that Gordimer has staged one. Chettle contends that revolutions "are messy things to write about, so perhaps [Gordimer] can be forgiven for being brief and somewhat vague about the revolution itself. She prefers to tell about a white family … [But] because her people think more than they feel, Miss Gordimer never seems to grapple seriously with the questions she has raised. The situation may be revolutionary but the insights are not." Another review in the *The Natal Witness* described Gordimer as a difficult prophet. Evidently, the narrative structure was too problematic.

Academic studies of Gordimer have been consistently insightful. They pick up on the myths being exploited in the novel while understanding the political play. Stephen Clingman, a fellow countryman, published *The Novels of Nadine Gordimer* after the 1985 State of Emergency—an admittance by the government that the nation was in a de facto state of civil war. He, therefore, offers particularly valuable insight. He writes:

> "in terms of the method in which its picture of revolution is presented, the novel is still candidly impressionistic. For there may be a way in which the novel is less interested in the future *per se* than in

> its unfolding in the present.... [thus the novel] may be the most deceptive, and deceptively simple, of all of Gordimer's novels, and perhaps less genuinely prophetic than, say, The Conservationist. What the novel is apparently doing is projecting a vision into the future; but what it may be doing most decisively is in fact the reverse. For what appears to be a projection from the present into the future in the novel is from another point of view *seeing the present through the eyes of the future* ..."

Change in South Africa, according to Clingman reading Gordimer, is inevitable but "nothing new has been born." And that is why the ambiguity of the novel's end is fitting.

Rowland Smith, in his 1990 essay, focuses on the frequency of impasse as a theme of Gordimer's works and the way *July's People* shatters this deadlock. Instead of stalled and hesitant whites confused about how to behave toward blacks, the whole of white society is blown away: " ... the collapse of white military power which the novel assumes is far less disturbing than the collapse of white moral power which it analyses. Part of the degradation of white suzerainty is shown to be white scruples themselves, even the scruples of human, dissenting whites. The paradox which epitomizes the deadlock of the book's ending is that only when the black man refuses to talk the white woman's language is she able to understand 'everything.'"

Kathrin Wagner's recent book, *Rereading Nadine Gordimer*, discusses many features of the novel. One element she focuses on is the "bildungsroman" element; that is, she watches Maureen's journey through a "heart of darkness" as one of self-discovery. Her journey, moreover, is that of a person in the "anguish of the only partially redeemed as history catches up with them." In such a reading, the run towards the helicopter—sign of civilization, technology, or the larger movements of history—with its complimentary baptismal dip in the river, becomes a simple reflex. Aware of the shallowness of her former life and, therefore, feeling even more out of place in the village, she seizes the moment and flees.

Still, according to Wagner, the novel falls apart at the end. "In her writing," says Wagner, "she implicitly and explicitly urges onward a historical process whose revolutionary phase must destroy the comfortable contexts within which she writes."

What Do I Read Next?

- Gordimer won the Booker Prize for her 1974 novel *The Conservationist.* The novel fictionalizes the consciousness of the agricultural settlers in South Africa and sets up the question being answered in *Burger's Daughter* and *July's People.* The question is, what role will whites have in the future of South Africa?
- *Burger's Daughter*, also by Gordimer (1979), won several awards but was banned in South Africa. It is the story of a woman very much the opposite of Maureen Smales. She is Rosa Burger, the daughter of Lionel Burger (a fictionalization of Abram Fischer—a

very prominent leader of the South African Communist Party), whose self-liberation from familial restraints requires acceptance of her political inheritance and challenges apartheid. One of the sources for this novel was Joe Slovo's 1976 essay, "South Africa-No Middle Road".

- *July's People* has often been compared to *Waiting for the Barbarians* (1980), by J.M. Coetzee, because of similar questions about the fate of those in power. Coetzee's story is a parable about colonialism told by the magistrate of a fort. A garrison has come to help defend the fort against unseen barbarians. Eventually, the garrison retreats and things return to normal, but it's unclear whether anyone will survive the coming winter or when the barbarians will attack.
- When the crackdown on dissent came in the 1960s in the wake of the ANC ban, Ruth First was one of the first to be imprisoned. She wrote about her experience in a novel called *117 Days* (1965). She was assassinated by letter bomb in 1982 and was survived by her husband, who was living in exile, Joe Slovo.
- Gordimer's novel makes constant

mention of health problems. Randall M. Pakard's 1990 work, *White Plague, Black Labor: Tuberculosis and the Political Economy of Health and Disease in South Africa (Comparative Studies of Health Systems and M)*, discusses the daunting health problems of South Africa.

- G. H. L. Le May's 1995 work, *The Afrikaners: An Historical Interpretation*, attempts to put some perspective on the people known as Afrikaners and their political system known as apartheid. He does so with hindsight and from a new South Africa.
- In 1987, Universal Pictures released a film, entitled *Cry Freedom*, about the events which led South Africans to suspect that a revolution was imminent. Denzel Washington played Steve Biko and Kevin Kline played Donald Woods, the editor of the *Daily Dispatch.*

Sources

Judith Chettle, in a review in *National Review*, Vol. XXXIII, No. 25, December, 1981, p. 1561.

Stephen Clingman, "The Subject of Revolution: Burger's Daughter and July's People," in *The Novels of Nadine Gordimer: History from the Inside*, Allen & Unwin, 1986, pp. 170-204.

Joan Silber, in a review in *New York Review of Books*, August, 1981, p. 14.

Rowland Smith, "Masters and Servants Nadine Gordimer's *July's People* and the Themes of Her Fiction," in *Critical Essays on Nadine Gordimer*, edited by Rowland Smith, G. K. Hall & Co., pp. 140-52.

Anne Tyler, "South Africa After the Revolution," in *New York Review of Books*, June, 1981, p. 26.

Kathrin Wagner, *Rereading Nadine Gordimer*, Indiana University Press, 1994, pp. 41, 5.

For Further Study

Michael Atwell, *South Africa: Background to the Crisis*, Sidgwick & Jackson, 1986.

With a splendid glossary, maps, and some photos, Atwell gives a general history of South Africa beginning with its exploration by whites from 1652.

Rosemarie Bodenheimer, "The Interregnum of Ownership in *July's People,"* in *The Later Fiction of Nadine Gordimer*, edited by Bruce King, St. Martin's, 1993, pp. 108-20.

Analyzes Gordimer's portrayal of the meaning and power of ownership, which for the characters defines political consciousness and identity.

Stephen Clingman, *The Novels of Nadine Gordimer: History from the Inside*, University of Massachusetts Press, 1986.

In his thorough study of Gordimer's novels, Clingman addresses the political, economic, linguistic, and sexual revolutions in *July's People* and connects the work to the historical moment in which it was composed.

Joseph Conrad, *The Heard of Darkness*, Beckwood's, 1899.

Conrad's novella is the parable of colonial empire. It is just one of the many colonial myths referenced in Gordimer's work.

John Cooke, "'Nobody's Children': Families in Gordimer's Later Novels," in *The Later Fiction of Nadine Gordimer*, edited by Bruce King, St. Martin's, 1993, pp. 21-32.

Concentrating on three Gordimer novels, Cooke discusses children's breaks from parental authority and the political significance of these breaks.

Daniel Defoe, *The Life and Adventures of Robinson Crusoe*, edited by Angus Ross, Penguin USA, 1995.

The famous tale of a shipwrecked man who survives for decades on an island. He constructs a settlement with his man Friday and dies very rich. The story came to epitomize the saga of the settler attempting to recreate England everywhere in the world.

Stefanie Dojka, "*July's People:* She Knew No Word," in *Joinings and Disjoinings: The Signifcance of Marital Status in Literature*, edited by JoAnna Stephens Mink and Janet Doubler Ward, Popular, 1991, pp. 155-71.

Traces the South African revolution's effects on the Smales' marriage and on Maureen Smales' changing character.

Lars Engle, "The Political Uncanny: The Novels of Nadine Gordimer," in *The Yale Journal of Criticism*, Vol. 2, No. 2, 1989, pp. 101-27.

Engle contrasts Gordimer's vision for South African art with that of Hendrik F. Verwoerd, former Prime Minister of South Africa, and he employs Freud's concept of the "uncanny" to analyze the political elements of Gordimer's fiction.

Nadine Gordimer, *The Essential Gesture: Writing, Politics and Places*, edited by Stephen Clingman, Alfred A. Knopf, 1988.

Collection of Gordimer's essays about her life, theory of writing, and political events relevant to her work.

Jennifer Gordon, "Dreams of a Common Language: Nadine Gordimer's *July's People,*" in *African Literature Today*, Vol. 15, 1987, pp. 102-08.

Gordon analyzes Gordimer's treatment of the power and limitations of language. She contends that Gordimer implies that a "common language" will be necessary to foster understanding between white and black South Africans.

Robert Green, "From *The Lying Days* to *July's*

People: The Novels of Nadine Gordimer," in *Journal of Modern Literature*, Vol. 14, No. 4, spring, 1988, pp. 543-63.

Green discusses Gordimer's artistic project, which records the changing consciousness of her time and intentionally challenges both her readers and herself.

Susan M. Greenstein, "Miranda's Story: Nadine Gordiner and the Literature of Empire," in *Novel: A Forum on Fiction*, Vol. 18, No. 3, spring, 1985, pp. 227-42.

Using the figures of Miranda and Caliban from Shakespeare's *The Tempest*, Greenstein examines two Gordimer novels and their breaks from traditional adventure literature about Africa.

Dominic Head, *Nadine Gordimer*, Cambridge University Press, 1994.

Traces major themes and issues throughout Gordimer's body of work and discusses the issues of identity in *July's People.*

Tom Lodge and Bill Nasson, *All, Here, and Now: Black Politics in South Africa in the 1980s*, Ford Foundation-Foreign Policy Association, 1991.

Explains the complex development of politics in the last decade of apartheid. Some background is given but its focus is on the events leading up to a negotiated end of white rule in South Africa.

Alan Paton, *Cry, The Beloved Country*, Twayne Publishing, 1991.

Set after World War II, the novel tells of the journey of man to the big city to find his son. The novel brought international attention to apartheid.

Sheila Roberts, "Sites of Paranoia and Taboo: Lessing's *The Grass Is Singing* and Gordimer's *July's People,"* in *Research in African Literatures*, Vol. 23, No. 3, fall, 1993, pp. 73-85.

Exploring the gothic devices in Lessing's and Gordimer's novels, Roberts views the dwellings the female protagonists inhabit as extensions of these women and, thus, "configurations of the uncanny."

Rowland Smith, "Masters and Servants: Nadine Gordimer's *July's People* and the Themes of Her Fiction," in *Critical Essays on Nadine Gordimer*, edited by Rowland Smith, Hall, 1990, pp. 140-52.

Connects *July's People* to Gordimer's earlier work, focusing on both the Smales' inability to escape their status as whites in July's village and the failures of communication between Maureen Smales and July.

Barbara Temple-Thurston, "Madam and Boy: A Relationship of Shame in Gordimer's *July's People,"* in *World Literature Written in English*, Vol. 28, No. 1, spring, 1988, pp. 51-8.

> Examines the breakdown of culturally determined roles in the novel, particularly the gendered relationship of "Madam" and "boy" between Maureen and July.

Andre Viola, "Communication and Liberal Double Bind in *July's People* by Nadine Gordimer," in *Commonwealth Essays and Studies*, Vol. 9, No. 2, spring, 1987, pp. 52-8.

> Referring to Paul Watzlawick's *Pragmatics of Human Communication*, Viola discusses the communication strategies that Gordimer depicts in the novel.

Nicholas Visser, "Beyond the Interregnum: A Note on the Ending of *July's People,"* in *Rendering Things Visible: Essays on South African Literary Culture*, edited by Martin Trump, Ohio University Press, 1990, pp. 61-7.

> Visser explores connections between the novel's ending and W. B. Yeats's "Leda and the Swan."

Kathrin Wagner, *Rereading Nadine Gordimer*, Indiana University Press, 1994.

> Examines Gordimer's political views, stereotypes, depictions of women

and black South Africans, and use of landscape iconography in her novels.

Printed in the USA
CPSIA information can be obtained
at www.ICGtesting.com
CBHW051917070724
11256CB00008B/347

9 781375 382885